THE FUTURE OF TRADITIONS

WRITING PICTURES: CONTEMPORARY ART FROM THE MIDDLE EAST

EDITED BY ROSE ISSA & BOB ANNIBALE

THE FUTURE OF TRADITIONS

THE WRITING OF ART

This exhibition, along with its catalogue, is about three generations of artists from Iran and the Arab world, from the early pioneers of a vernacular Lettrism movement in the 1960s till now. It includes a few exceptional contemporary calligraphers, but mainly those only occasionally incorporating the written word in their works today. These artists, from different backgrounds and possessing diverse styles, take inspiration from their own culture; they use the morphology of letters and phonemes, the rhymes and rhythms of calligraphy, abstracting words into pictures and thoughts into images. The result over the past six decades has been the creation of an alternative and original approach to modernism and contemporary art, while representing the birth of new and different aesthetics.

Partly based on the book *Signs of Our Times: From Calligraphy to Calligraffiti* (2016), the exhibition includes artists whose concerns, whether conceptual, socio-political or simply aesthetic, have found their own modes of expression, thus making a distinctive contribution to world art. For, as Oscar Wilde remarked, "Be yourself; everyone else is already taken."

From the thirty-seven artists represented here, only a very few are calligraphers (Mohammad Ehsaey, Ahmed Moustafa, Hassan Massoudy, Mouneer al-Shaarani and Joumana Medlej). The exhibition offers a glimpse into a variety of contemporary art approaches using Persian and Arabic scripts, while introducing the work of some younger-generation women artists like Hanieh Delecroix, Parastou Forouhar, Farnaz Jahanbin, Katayoun Rouhi, or the architect and sculptor Nayla Romanos Iliya, who gives innovative shapes to the Phoenician alphabet, the base of many languages from Arabic to Latin. You can notice several instances of *La'* (No) in Ali Omar Ermes or Said Baalbaki's

MALIHEH AFNAN
TABLET, PLASTER OF PARIS AND WATER BASED PAINT, 21 X 29 CM, 1995

work, as to NO to injustice, to double standards; Mahmoud Obaidi's *Salam*, made of swords, hints to how peace can be achieved, or not, through war. As for Mahmoud Bakhshi, his work criticising the commercialisation of calligraphy is painted in a beautiful Persian script!

Providing a window into the infinitely variable interpretations and articulations of the art of writing, the exhibition examines the plasticity between word, idea and image. The works create a moving dialogue of visual poetry that implicitly weaves culture and history with the ineffable and the sublime.

Using richly varied vocabularies of art – painting or sculpting the words, or creating 'artist books', and whether bringing peace to war, rebellion to confront double standards, or poetry to overcome malaise – they offer a fresh perspective on the creativity that the region has inspired.

For educational purposes we have incorporated selected manuscripts from the hidden treasures of the Special Collections of the School of Oriental and African Studies' Library. There are 9th-century Kufic parchments, 16th-century Safavid gilded poetry and 18th-century specimens of calligraphic Mashq in concertina books. There is even a 12-13th century Seljuk cobalt-blue-glazed ewer, probably from Kashan. These precious items from the past are now in dialogue with the contemporary works in this exhibition.

My very special thanks to: Bob Annibale, my co-editor and co-curator; the artists for their contributions; the collectors for lending the works; the sponsors for making it possible; Petra Kottmair and Francesca Ricci for producing this catalogue; and John Hollingworth from Brunei Gallery for its patient support.

ROSE ISSA
GUEST CURATOR

ALI OMAR ERMES
LA', THE POSITIVE NO
MIXED MEDIA ON PAPER
30 X 36 CM, 1989

ARTISTS

RACHID KORAICHI

AHMED MOUSTAFA

NJA MAHDAOUI

MALIHEH AFNAN

SIAH ARMAJANI

MOHAMMAD EHSAEY

JUMANA BAYAZID EL HUSSEINI

MOUNEER AL SHAARAWI

HASSAN MASSOUDY

HOSSEIN VALAMANESH

ENAYATOLLAH NOURI

ALI OMAR ERMES

ETEL ADNAN

SHAKIR HASSAN AL SAID

MEHDI QOTBI

HALIM AL KARIM

FARHAD MOSHIRI

KHALED BEN SLIMANE

FATHI HASSAN

BITA GHEZELAYAGH

FARNAZ JAHANBIN

MANAL AL DOWAYAN

FARHAD AHRARNIA

WALID SITI

PARASTOU FOROUHAR

MAHMOUD OBAIDI

SAID BAALBAKI

SUSAN HEFUNA

NAYLA ROMANOS ILIYA

CHANT AVEDISSIAN

MAHMOUD BAKHSHI

NASSER AL ASWADI

KATAYOUN ROUHI

RACHID KORAICHI

ALGERIA/FRANCE (B.1947)

Artist, painter, sculptor and humanist, Rachid Koraichi has, in the past five decades, created works and projects in collaboration with poets, writers and craftspeople that he calls his *'magiciens'*. His architectural works, gardens of memories, pay homage to leaders such as Emir Abdelkader, or unknown migrants drowned in the Mediterranean (*Jardin d'Afrique, Zarzis*).

UNTITLED
MIXED MEDIA ON PAPER, 110 X 220 CM, 1981

FROM THE SERIES **LE SEPT STATIONS CÉLESTES**
SOFT PASTE PORCELAIN, BLUE AND WHITE OXIDE, 50 X 47 X 47 CM, 2018
COURTESY OF OCTOBER GALLERY, LONDON

AHMED MOUSTAFA

EGYPT/UK (B.1943)

Moustafa is an Egyptian-born artist and scholar of international repute and now a leading authority on Arabic art and design. He has lived and worked in London since 1974 and directs the Fe-Noon Ahmed Moustafa Research Centre for Arab Art and Design, which he established in 1983. His work is now almost exclusively devoted to abstract compositions inspired by texts from the Holy Qur'an. He has created an astonishingly rich visual vocabulary through an innovative fusion of his skills as a painter and as a master scribe in the tradition of Islamic penmanship.

WHEN THE TWO OCEANS MEET
LIMITED EDITION IRIS PRINT, 127 X 160 CM, 2003

THE CUBE is a "multiple" of a sculpture by Dr Ahmed Moustafa. **THE HIDDEN DIMENSION OF THE CUBE** comprises a book entitled **THE ATTRIBUTES OF DIVINE PERFECTION** and its three-dimensional depiction represented by **THE CUBE** itself. When the cube is open, 99 cubic units are revealed, each of which bears a "Divine Attribute" written in square-Kufic script.**THE HIDDEN DIMENSION OF THE CUBE** is made of synthetic resin. The golden parts, representing the Attributes, are laminated with twenty-four carat gold. The dimension of the closed cube is 167 x 167 x 167 mm. When the sculpture is opened, the height of The Cube is 317.3 mm.

NJA MAHDAOUI

TUNISIA (B.1937)

Known as the choreographer of letters, Mahdaoui has been shaping the morphology of letters for over four decades, without us being able to decipher a word. His love of music, dance and poetry have given his calligrams – whether on parchment, paper, textile or bronze – a distinctive shape and signature.

CALLIGRAM
INK ON PARCHMENT, 100 X 140 CM, 1990

BANDERA
SOLVENT ON DENIM, 160 X 700 CM, 1995

MALIHEH AFNAN

IRAN/ FRANCE (1935-2016)

Afnan's work – mostly on paper, with layers of earth colours, browns, black and rust – comes from a variety of influences: her love of old manuscripts and ancient scrolls, her upbringing in Palestine, her Eastern cultures and her education and later life in the Western world. Most of her work represents undecipherable imagined writings.

CONTAINED THOUGHTS
NINE WORKS, MIXED MEDIA ON PAPER, VARIOUS SIZES, 21-39 CM HIGH, 10 CM DIAMETER, 2000

SIAH ARMAJANI
IRAN/USA (1939-2020)

An Iranian-born American sculptor and architect, Armajani is better known for his public art, bridges and more political work, from the large sculptural installation of *Rooms of Hospitality* for anarchists and exiles to the glass room *Fallujah*, another masterpiece. This work is a much earlier one, using writings in Farsi.

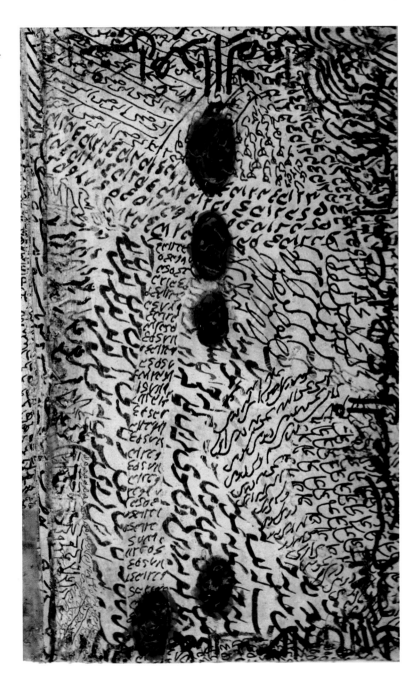

LETTER
MIXED MEDIA ON TEXTILE, 26.5 X 17.5 CM, 1960

MOHAMMAD EHSAEY

IRAN (B.1939)

Ehsaey is a calligrapher and designer, whose stylised work is characterised by a melding of Persian calligraphy, graphic design and Modernist abstraction. Two-tone compositions of conflated Arabic symbols and script, painted on large-scale canvases, form the backbone of Ehsaey's practice.

MOHEBBAT (KINDNESS)
OIL ON CANVAS. 130 X 130 CM, 2006

JUMANA BAYAZID EL HUSSEINI

PALESTINE/ FRANCE (1932-2018)

El Husseini chose to seek refuge in the harmonious, colourful cities of her Palestinian dreamscapes and, later on, embroidery and tapestry work; in the final decade of her life she used much darker shades and contrasting colours. Her work reflects distant memories, creating an atmosphere of fragility and tenderness.

UNTITLED FROM THE **BLACK** SERIES
MIXED MEDIA ON PAPER, 75 X 60 CM, 1999

MOUNEER AL SHAARANI

SYRIA (B.1952)

Al-Shaarani is a Syrian graphic artist specialising in Arabic calligraphy. He is known as calligrapher, graphic designer and author of articles about Arabic calligraphy and Arab Islamic art. He has designed several Arabic typefaces for book covers or other graphic creations.

NO SOUL SHOULD BEAR THE WEIGHT OF ANOTHER
GOUACHE ON PAPER, 110 X 110 CM, 2016. ARTIST COLLECTION/MANAS GHANEM

HASSAN MASSOUDY
IRAQ (B. 1944)

Massoudy, who currently lives in Paris and has published several books on his work there, is an Iraqi painter and calligrapher. He uses international proverbs and sayings in the works that best represent his humanistic approach to life. His art has influenced a generation of calligraffiti artists.

THE WORKING BEE HAS NO TIME FOR SORROW, (WILLIAM BLAKE), INK ON PAPER, 75 X 55 CM, 2009
TO TRUST IS A SIGN OF COURAGE, (MARIA VAN EBNET ESCHENBACK, 1830-1916), INK ON PAPER, 75 X 55 CM, 2009

HOSSEIN VALAMANESH

IRAN/AUSTRALIA (1949-2022)

Valamanesh was an Iranian-Australian contemporary artist who lived and worked in Adelaide, South Australia. He worked in mixed media, printmaking, installations and sculpture. He often collaborated with his wife, Angela Valamanesh, and his son Nassiem, the video artist. His refined and relevant work can be seen in the majority of Australian museums.

THIS WILL ALSO PASS I PUISQUE TOUT PASSE
BRONZE, 70 CM, 2012

HEECH MAGOU (DON'T SAY ANYTHING)
BRONZE, 55 X 44 CM, 2004. COLLECTION INA SARIKHANI SANDMAN, LONDON

ENAYATOLLAH NOURI

IRAN (B. 1937)

Iranian poet and calligrapher.

 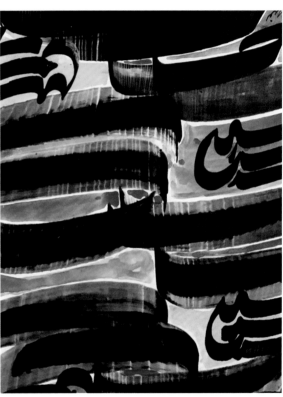

OF LETTERS
MIXED MEDIA ON PAPER, 44 X 39 CM AND 37 X 32 CM, 2003

ALI OMAR ERMES

LIBYA/UK (1945-2021)

The paintings of Ermes, a Libyan British artist and poet, incorporate Maghrebi script, often superimposed on a rich-textured ground, and may include fragments of old Arabic or contemporary poetry or prose. Most of his painting is about secular words.

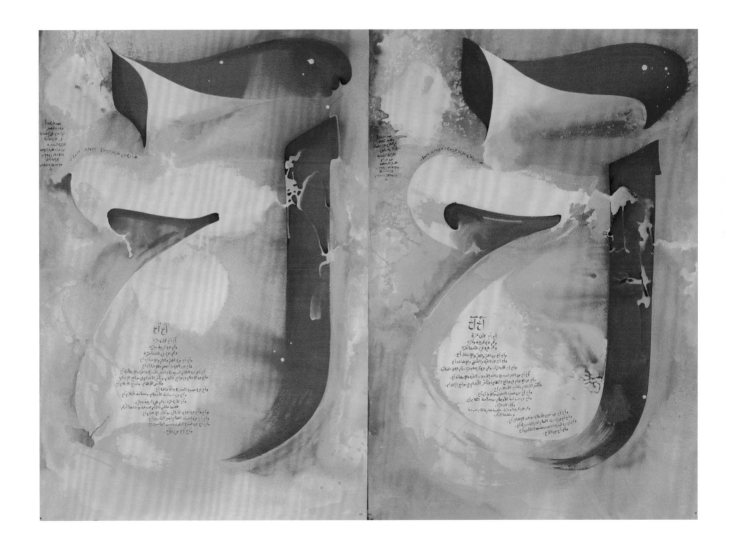

AAKHIN-AAKH KAMAN MARA (AGAIN AND AGAIN AAHH!)
DIPTYCH, ACRYLIC AND INK ON PAPER 208 X 154 EACH, 2014. COLLECTION ESTATE OF ALI OMAR ERMES

ETEL ADNAN

SYRIA/LEBANON/FRANCE (1925-2021)

Known for her poetry, novels and plays, Adnan produced visual works in a variety of media, such as oil paintings, concertina books and tapestries. A multi-linguist who had a nomadic existence, she moved fluidly between writing and art and was a leading voice of contemporary Arab culture.

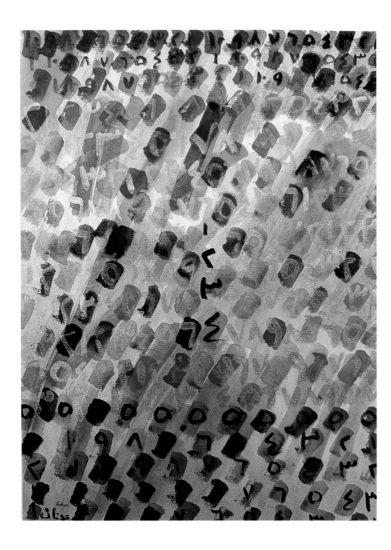

UNTILED FROM THE **MYSTERIOUS NUMBERS** SERIES, MIXED MEDIA ON PAPER 65 X 50 CM, 1992. COLLECTION BOB ANNIBALE AND EDESIO FERNANDES

SHAKIR HASSAN AL SAID
IRAQ (1925–2004)

Considered one of Iraq's most innovative and influential painters and sculptors, Al Said was also a philosopher, an art critic and an art historian who shaped the modern Iraqi art movement and connected modernity and heritage. His theories charted a new Arabic art aesthetic, with his use of frequently mysterious and mystical numbers often replacing words and letters.

UNTITLED
MIXED MEDIA ON PAPER, 61 X 73.4 CM, 1979

MEHDI QOTBI

MOROCCO (B. 1951)

Mehdi Qotbi defines himself as being 'engaged in an act of unwriting'; incorporating signs, scriptural shapes, patterns to 'fill in emptiness'. He brings together the artistic resources of writing and the visual expressiveness of shapes, transforming writing into painting, characters into patterns.

UNTITLED
LITHOGRAPH, 67 X 50 CM, 1994

HALIM AL KARIM
IRAQ (B. 1963)

Halim al-Karim spent almost three years hiding in the desert to oppose compulsory military service under Saddam Hussein's regime in the first Gulf War. During his self-exile, al-Karim was exposed to mysticism, magic and Gypsy culture. This valuable experience was a source of inspiration behind the artist's work, which blurs divisions between light and dark, permanent and temporary, reality and mysticism.

UNTITLED
ACRYLIC ON CANVAS, 99 X 99 CM, 2007

FARHAD MOSHIRI
IRAN (B.1963)

Farhad Moshiri's mixed-media practice spans painting, assemblage and sculpture. He is inspired by Pop Art and conceptualism. His hybrid aesthetics are at the crossroads of the Middle East and the West. These earlier works, paintings of monumental jars from the *Reservoirs of Memory* series, are impressive containers of desire and eulogies to the simple pleasures of life. Variations on the theme of a humble vessel are rendered in colours that he associates with particular words, sentences or childhood memories.

GREETINGS TO YOU, OH MORNING
MIXED MEDIA ON CANVAS, 203 X 162.5 CM, 2003
COLLECTION SAEB AND FARIBA EIGNER

NIGHTINGALE BIRD/HUMMING BIRD IN THE GRASS
MIXED MEDIA ON CANVAS, APPROX. 209 X 166 CM, 2003
COLLECTION SAEB AND FARIBA EIGNER

KHALED BEN SLIMANE
TUNISIA, (B. 1951)

Mostly famous as a ceramicist, Khaled Ben Slimane works in a multi-disciplinary practice that includes paintings on paper, canvas and wood as well as bronze sculptures. A synthesis of East and West, his work invokes Sufism through graphic repetition of words and phrases in a distinctive style.

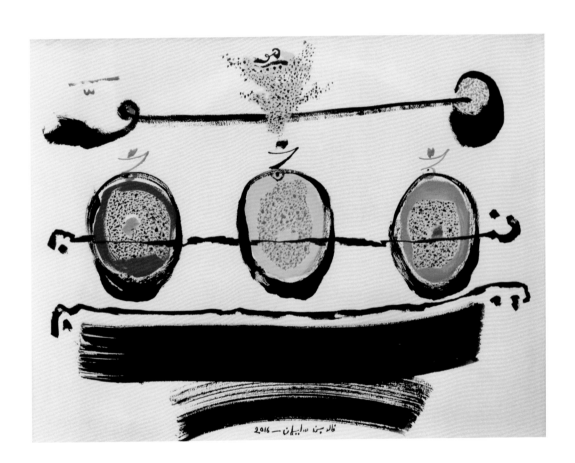

ASCENSION IV
ACRYLIC ON ARCHES PAPER, 50.4 X 66 CM, 2016.
COLLECTION CESTAR

FATHI HASSAN

EGYPT/ITALY (B.1957)

Hassan's work often emphasizes power dynamics and the relationship between the oral and written word; drawing from his Nubian heritage, he places particular emphasis on the loss of language under the dominance of colonialism. Most of his scripts remain deliberately illegible and impossible to decipher. As here in *Haram Aleikum* (Shame on You), his concerns are socio-political: why do you do what you are doing, say what you are saying?

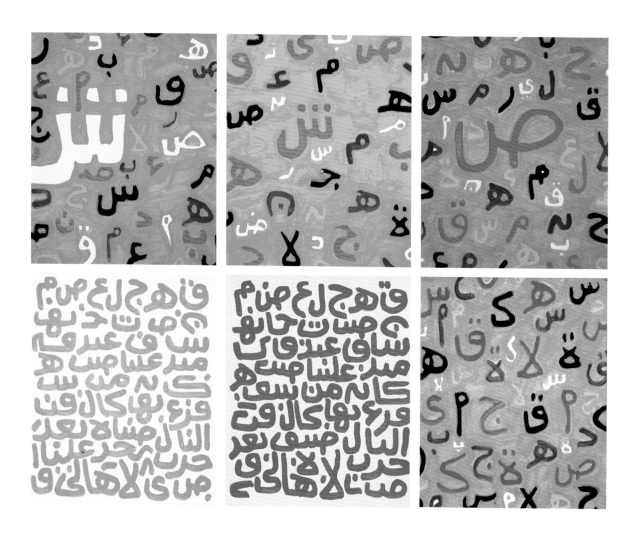

FROM THE SERIES **LETTERS**
MIXED MEDIA ON CARD, 32 X 27 CM, 1985–1995

HARAM ALEIKUM
MIXED MEDIA ON PAPER, 150 X 100 CM, 2010

BITA GHEZELAYAGH

IRAN/UK (B.1966)

Previously an architect, Ghezelayagh has worked with media such as felt, combining talismanic symbols, silk-screen printing and embroidery. She has sought a new visual language that embraces tradition and modernity through ancient signs, symbols and calligraphy in a unique combination with conceptual art.

SIX ELEMENTS
FROM THE **LOVERS OF APADANA** SERIES, MIXED MEDIA, METAL, TEXTILE AND INKS
6 X 16 CM EACH – 32 X 48 CM TOTAL SIZE, 2018

FARNAZ JAHANBIN
IRAN (B. 1966)

Jahanbin, a singer and painter based in Tehran, here shapes some of the key words she sings, such as: Nazdik (Near); Yek Digar (Each Other), Pass (So); Khodam (Myself); Waqe'i (Real); Tekrar (Repeat); Sokout (Silence); Derakht (Tree); Chera (Why).

10 WORDS
INSTALLATION OF TEN WORKS, MIXED MEDIA ON CANVAS STUCK ON BOARD
36 X 26 CM EACH, 2015

MANAL AL DOWAYAN
SAUDI ARABIA (B. 1973)

Best known for her black-and-white photographic work or her installation piece *Suspended Together*, al-Dowayan always pinpoints women's rights, by interrogating the gender-biased customs that impact the condition of women in Saudi Arabia. In her practice the personal and the political overlap. *Just Paper*, in silk-screen on porcelain with jute string, features a text taken from a 10th-century Arabic book by Abu Mansour al Tha'alabi (961–1038).

JUST PAPER
SILKSCREEN ON PORCELAIN WITH JUTE STRING
SCROLLS DIMENSIONS VARIABLE, 2021–2022

FARHAD AHRARNIA

IRAN/UK (B. 1971)

Ahrarnia is a prolific multi-media artist who produces his works between Shiraz and Shieffield, using films, documents, embroidery, silverwork and printing technique. In this series, *Death in America*, made in 2011, by changing just one letter from B to D ('Marg bar Amrika' to 'Marg dar Amrika') Ahrarnia reminds us of the deathly aspect of American history and identity, and the act of colonial construction of a nation.

BURY MY HEART V
DIGITAL PHOTOGRAPHY ON CANVAS
EMBROIDERY AND NEEDLES, 35.5 X 51.5 CM, 2011

WALID SITI
KURDISTAN/UK (B.1954)

Born in war-torn Dohuk, in Iraqi Kurdistan, Siti subverts the concept of monuments for the unknown soldier into a *Monument to the Unsung*, paying tribute to women, the strength of mothers, sisters, daughters and wives, who deal with the brunt of wars and conflicts. Shaped as a pyramid, the piece comprises fifty-five blocks engraved with Kurdish female names. Each block carries a different name, with their meanings derived from nature, like Kani (spring) or Ronahi (light).

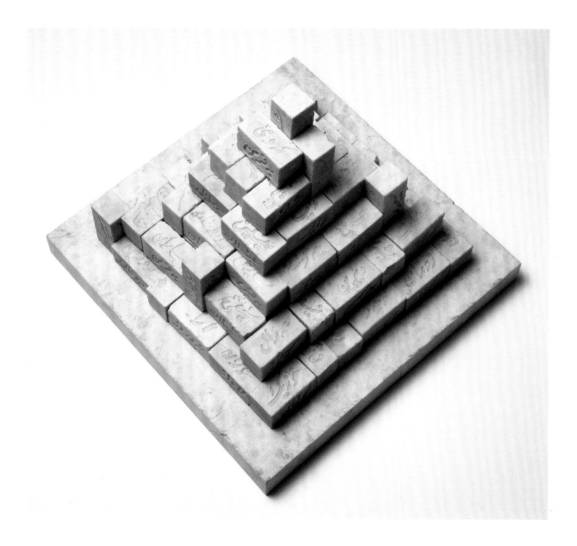

MONUMENT TO THE UNSUNG
MARBLE, 40 X 40 X 40 CM, 2016

PARASTOU FOROUHAR
IRAN/GERMANY (B.1962)

Installation artist Forouhar expresses in most of her work her critical response towards the politics in Iran and Islamic fundamentalism. Her largely autobiographical work draws on the loss of her parents, Dariush and Parvaneh Forouhar, with subtle references opposing violence and political crimes. In this series, the *Persian Alphabet*, based on her earlier drawings when she was challenged to be more Iranian than conceptual, she combines humour, skill and old traditional zoomorphic calligraphy.

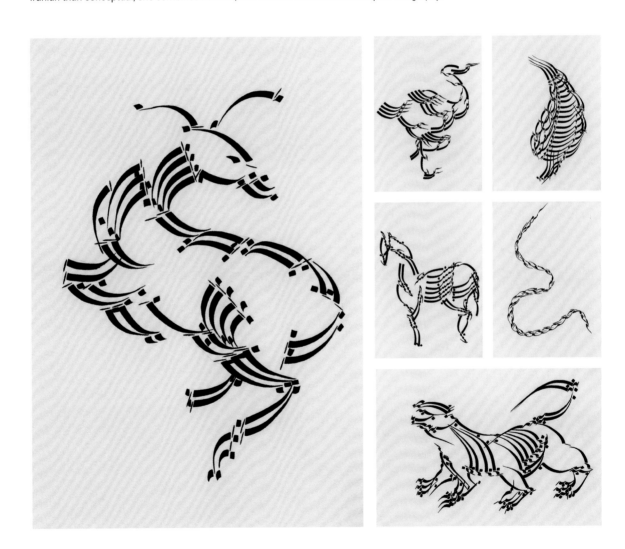

PERSIAN FOR BEGINNERS
SET OF 12 PRINTS, 40 X 30 CM, 1997–2012

MAHMOUD OBAIDI

IRAQ (B.1966)

Obaidi is a multimedia Iraqi-Canadian artist, filmmaker and architect, who has always shown a radical, critical social understanding. From *The Imposter*, or the *Replacement*, at the Venice Biennale (*In the Eye of the Thunderstorm: Effervescent Practices from the Arab World, 2015*), to his *Farewell Kiss*, representing George W. Bush surrounded by shoes, to his museum in north Lebanon, he has proved his unrivalled courage, talent and political commitments.

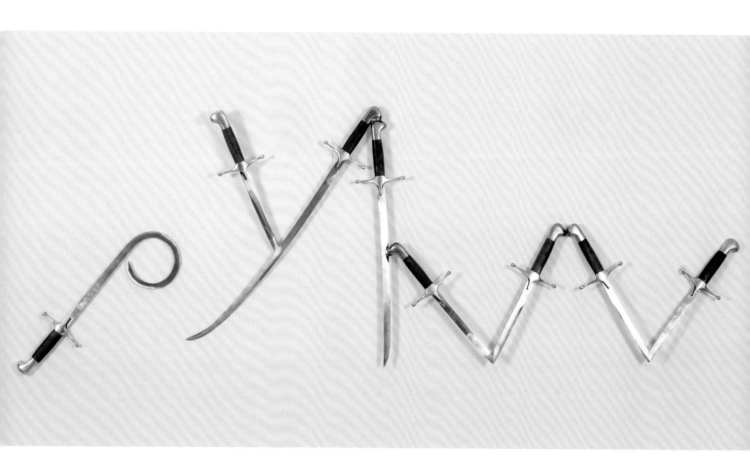

SALAM
FROM THE **CONFUSIONISM** SERIES, STEEL AND WOOD, 230 X 73 X 3 CM, 2013. COLLECTION SHAMIYANA, LONDON

SAID BAALBAKI
LEBANON/GERMANY/ (B. 1974)

Baalbaki and his family were often uprooted and forced to move between different districts in Beirut and elsewhere in Lebanon during the war. He is now based in Berlin. His paintings, often devoid of people, portray piles of items such as suitcases or other belongings, symbolising lost, unrecorded and forgotten stories of history. His more conceptual work seeks to challenge the credibility of museums and institutions, asking: 'Why and how does an artefact presented in a museum convey the impression of utmost credibility and authenticity to the spectator?' Here using the letter 'La' (No) he conveys his objection to double standards and injustice.

LA' (NO)
BRONZE, 100 X 50 CM, 2018

SUSAN HEFUNA

EGYPT/GERMANY (B. 1962)

Hefuna is a German-Egyptian visual artist who works in a variety of media, including drawing, photography, sculpture, installation, video and performance. She achieved some recognition in the East and West through her drawings and screens (*mashrabiya*), incorporating Arabic, English and German key words. When she reached the age of forty-five, full recognition came to her. This work celebrates that year, with forty-five bronze metals repeating 'Patience is Beautiful,' a motto she has repeated in Arabic and English in many of her works.

DREAM, HELM
CAST BRONZE SILVER, 50 X 70 X 4 CM, 2009

NAYLA ROMANOS ILIYA

LEBANON (B. 1961)

Architect Romanos Iliya has used her sculptural skills and explored issues of identity, with its layers of history and aesthetical concerns. By simplifying inherited forms into semi-abstract minimal sculptures, she has created a personal poetic vision with her new interpretation of an ancient alphabet.

PHOENICIAN ALPHABET
BRONZE, VARIOUS DIMENSIONS, 2012—14

CHANT AVEDISSIAN

EGYPT (1951-2018)

Apart from his well-known *Icons of the Niles*, Chant Avedissian has worked from the geometry and design of the Silk Road, from China, via Japan to Egypt. Some of his stencil works refer to daily sayings: This too shall pass, or I put my trust into God...

THIS TOO WILL PASS
GOUACHE ON CARDBOARD, 50 X 70 CM, 2014

MAHMOUD BAKHSHI MOAKHAR

IRAN (B.1977)

Bakhshi's installations and sculptural works analyse the aesthetics of post-revolutionary Iran and industrial capitalism. His work represents an art that is self-conscious and questions the role and impact of an artist today, juxtaposed with the reflective nature and effect of an influential work of art on society. Here he emphasises the controversial role of those who exploit calligraphy to sell their art.

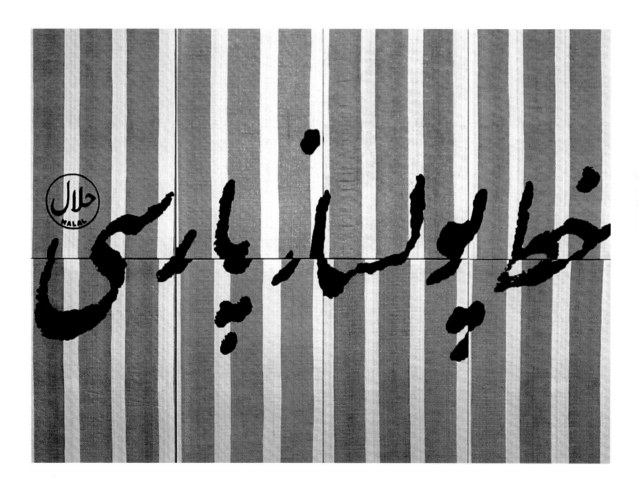

KHATE POOLSAZE PARSI (THE MONEY MAKING PERSIAN SCRIPT)
GUMI PLASTER, 200 X 240 CM, 2010. COLLECTION SHIRLEY ELGHANIAN

NASSER AL ASWADI

YEMEN/ FRANCE (B. 1978)

Al Aswadi, who studied architecture in Taiz and Sanaa, now lives in Marseille. For him calligraphy is a way to express feelings and thoughts beyond the realm of written language. Letters and words are not drawn out in their typical sequence, laid out in a straight line; instead, they are artfully painted and stacked separately, tangled and lost in an imaginary space. Al Aswadi's interlocking letters form a visual language that has exhausted the traditional styles of Arabic writing to create a new world in which his work touches the edges of abstraction.

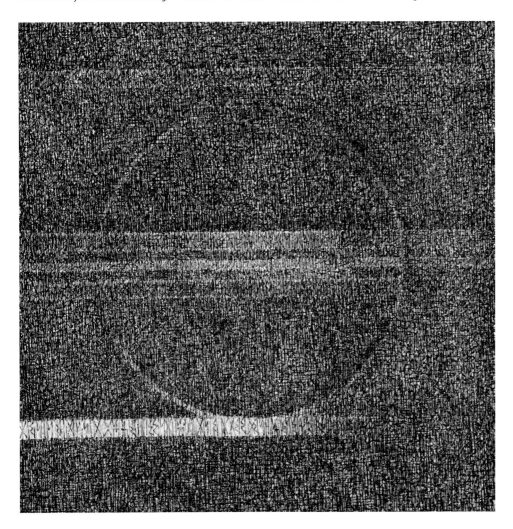

UNTITLED
OIL ON CANVAS, 135 X 135 CM, 2022

KATAYOUN ROUHI
IRAN/FRANCE (B. 1965)

Based in Paris, Rouhi has been painting and writing mainly autobiographical texts, upside down, combined with images of a young girl or trees to form her *Conference of the Birds* series. It is inspired by the 12th-century Persian Sufi poet Farid ud-Din Attar, commonly known as Attar of Nishapur.

LANGAGE DES OISEAUX
OIL ON CANVAS, 120 X 120 CM, 2012

ARTISTS BOOKS

ETEL ADNAN

HANIEH DELECROIX

KAMAL BOULLATA

CHRISTINE KHONDJIE

JOUMANA MEDLEJ

JACQUELINE BÉJANI

ETEL ADNAN
SYRIA/LEBANON/FRANCE (1925-2021)

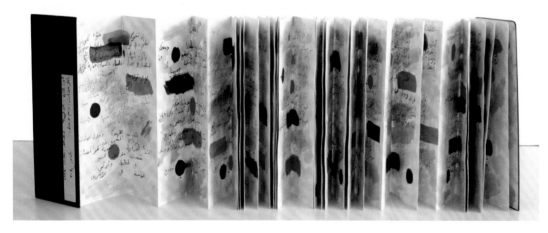

BADR SHAKER SAYYAB
LEPORELLO BOOK IN 30 PAGES, 27 X 9 CM, 1989

ONSI EL HAJJ
LEPORELLO BOOK, EACH PAGE 30 X 10.5 CM, 2004

HANIEH DELECROIX

IRAN/FRANCE (B. 1974)

Based in Paris, Hanieh Delecroix works as a psychologist, but most of her time is spent drawing, writing, making children's books and combining Persian or French writings with her dominant use of black and blue, both in her artwork and artist books.

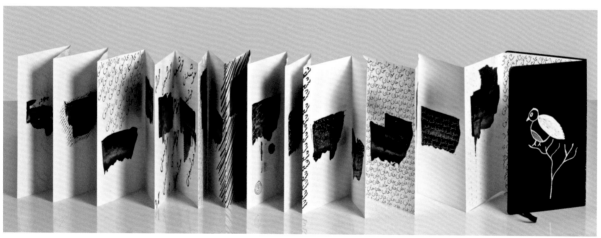

THE SONG OF THE POETS
INK ON PAPER, 21 X 13.5 CM, 2022

ALL THE FLOWERS KNOW THE STRENGTH OF THE WIND
INK ON PAPER, 21 X 13.5 CM, 2022

KAMAL BOULLATA
PALESTINE/USA (1942-2019)

A Palestinian artist and art historian, Boullata was known for work, abstract in style, primarily executed in acrylic, often focusing on the ideas of division in Palestinian identity and separation from homeland.

ADONIS, BEGINNINGS
ED 30/40, 1992

CHRISTINE KHONDJI

IRAN/FRANCE (B.1947)

'Books are rivers where flow my obsessions: prehistory, archaeology, and life.' Christine Khondji's artist books are based on collages, in particular the books of Gnawa, a Moroccan religious celebration, with songs, ritual poetry, traditional music and dancing, dedicated to prayer and healing, guided by the Gnawa master musician. Each spirit bears its own specific colour.

THE GNAWA BOOK
MIXED MEDIA, 21 X 14.5 CM, 2020-21

HAFEZ
MIXED MEDIA, 21 X 14.5 CM, 2020-21

JOUMANA MEDLEJ

LEBANON (B. 1979)

A designer based in London, Medlej studied under Samir Sayegh, a well-known Lebanese calligrapher. In the past five years, she has created several limited-edition artist's books: *A Pocketful of Love* (2018), with the words and variations expressing love; *The Book of the Moon* (2018), with cycles of the moon written in Arabic; or the much larger *Canticle of Creatures*, by St Francis of Assisi, written in traditional Arabic script (2021).

BOOK OF LOVE
11,5 X 11,5 CM (PAGE SIZE), 2018

THE BOOK OF THE MOON
WATERCOLOUR ON PAPER
5 X 11 X 2.5 CM (PAGE SIZE),
APPROX. 50 X 50 CM (OPEN), 2018

JACQUELINE BÉJANI
LEBANON/PALESTINE (B. 1959)

Living in Luxembourg, Béjani's leporello, *Beirut is One*, pays homage to Etel Adnan. Repeating Beirut's name like a mantra, she rediscovered the city through the long walks during the Covid era. She wrote the names of all the districts mixing them randomly, wanting to unify the divided areas, and gathered them using colours or stitching. The holes symbolize the destructions Beirut had to endure, the stitches the efforts to rebuild the heritage.

CONNECTING BEIRUT
MIXED MEDIA ON PAPER, EACH PAGE 21 X 13 CM, 2020

A SELECTION FROM THE SPECIAL COLLECTION OF OLD MANUSCRIPTS FROM THE LIBRARY OF SOAS

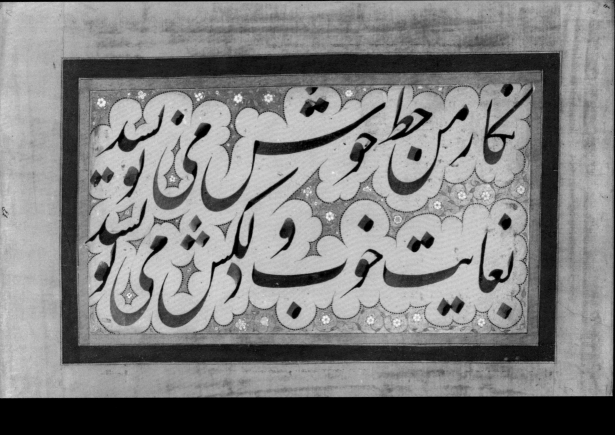

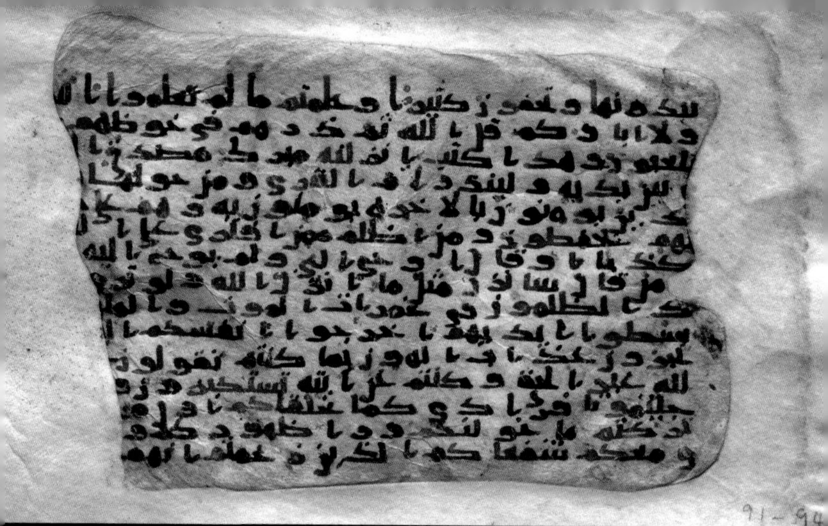

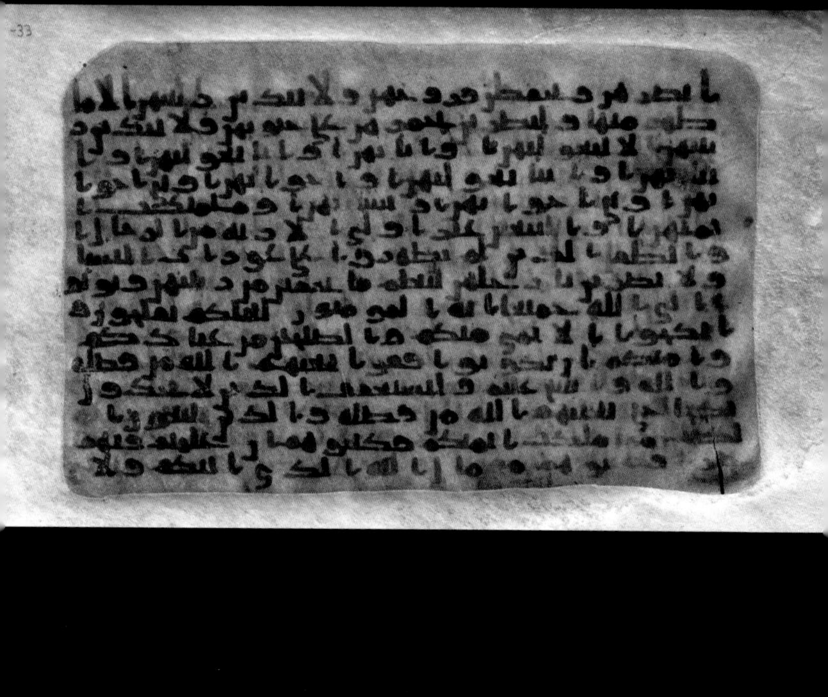

KUFIC QUR'AN ON PARCHMENT

CA. 9TH C. DETACHED LEAVES, WITH DIFFERENT SURAS FROM THE QUR'AN, BELONGING TO DIFFERENT HANDS. SPECIAL COLLECTIONS, SOAS LIBRARY, MS 199351

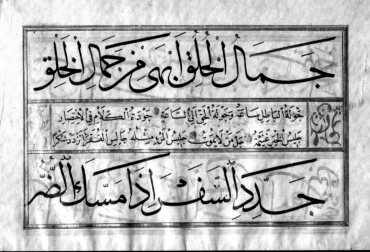

Two pages from a slim, leather-bound book, dated 1167 AH (1753-54 CE) produced in Ottoman Turkey. It contains a collection of Arabic maxims attributed to 'Ali, the Prophet Muhammad's son-in-law and fourth successor as caliph. These maxims enjoyed considerable popularity in the Muslim world and exist in many versions; this particular collection arranges the sayings alphabetically. The maxims are handsomely written in various scripts such as thuluth and naskh and arranged horizontally lengthwise; each page has four lines of text, the upper- and lowermost being larger in scale than those in between. Contadini, Anna (ed.), *Objects of Instruction. Treasures of the School of Oriental and African Studies*, London 2007, p. 105, no. 82.

از آب خود بر مدارشت مهرجو... آمله سیراب از پی آب آمد

Swahili is an Eastern African Bantu language with many Arabic elements acquired through contact with Arab traders since about 90 CE. The oldest transcriptions of oral Swahili poetry, written in Arabic script, are from the early 18th century. Poetry plays an important cultural role, encouraged by religious leaders whose Arabic verses may be paraphrased interlinearly in Swahili. Such poetry protect the individual and embodies patrician Swahili values of purity and piety, expressing pride in their Arab origins. Contadini, Anna (ed. *Objects of Instruction. Treasures of the School of Oriental and African Studies*, London 2007, p. 115, no. 90.

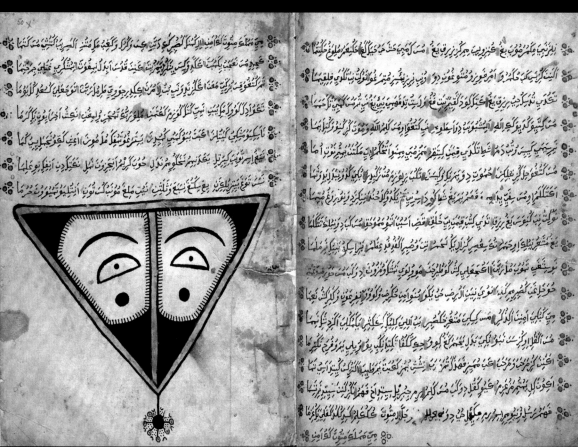

Badr-i Munir meeting Benazir. Mir Hasan, Masnavi or Sihr ul Bayan (The Enchanting Story). Urdu. Delhi School, India, early 19th century. Opaque watercolour, gold and ink on paper. H17.6cm xW9.9cm. MS 24931. Gift of Lt. -Col. D.C.Philott. fols.42v-43r. This Urdu poem was written by Mir Hasan in 1785 and dedicated to the ruler of Oudh Asaf ud-Daula (r.1775-97). The hero of the story is Benazir, who is captured by a Fairy on his twelfth birthday. He falls in love with the beautiful princess Badr-i Munir. After a painful separation the pair are finally reunited. This miniature (fo.42v) shows Badr-i Munir meeting Benazir, who has been watching the princess and her maidens. Contadini, Anna (ed.), *Objects of Instruction. Treasures of the School of Oriental and African Studie*s, London 2007, p. 77, no. 58.

The pages of this beautiful book were produced in 16th century Safavid Iran and contain a collection of 40 Arabic hadith – sayings of the Prophet Muhammad - compiled and paraphrased into Persian verse by the celebrated Iranian poet and mystic Jami (1414-92). Composed in 886 AH (1481 CE), Jami's text belonged to a flourishing and widespread tradition of hadith compilations. This particular copy is calligraphed in an elegant nasta'liq script and delicately illuminated throughout. Each page comprises a central panel of light-blue paper on which the text is written and a broad margin of scrolling blossoms rendered in gold paint. The book was provided in the first half of the 19th century with a fine lacquered cover painted with naturalistic flowers. Contadini, Anna (ed.), *Objects of Instruction. Treasures of the School of Oriental and African Studies*, London, 2007, p.101 no. 78.

Calligraphic Maghribi Arabic, literary/historical composition, illuminated throughout, describing the presentation of an Indian elephant, called Skoke, from Queen Victoria to Hassan I, Sutan of Morocco, 1873-1894, presented by Captain Inglewood in 1891.

AL-DURAR AL-SANIYAH FI AL-HADIYAH AL-WAFIDAH MIN FAKHIM AL-HADRAH AL-NAJLIZIYAH
BY BALGHITHI, AL-THAHIR IBN AHMAD. SPECIAL COLLECTIONS, SOAS LIBRARY. MS380279

LEFT: **ARBA'UN HADITHAN**
NUR AL-DIN 'ABD AL-RAHMAN JAMI, *ARBA'UN HADITHAN* (FORTY TRADITION). PERSIAN. SAFAVID IRAN, 16TH CENTURY, WATERCOLOUR, GOLD AND INK ON PAPER. H 24.2 X W 15.2 CM. SPECIAL COLLECTIONS, SOAS LIBRARY. MS 35343

The album, kept within a lacquer binding opens in concertina fashion and comprises 28 pages. Each page has bold floral margins, some inhabited by birds and insects, some executed in a characteristically Qajar style, which postdates the examples of calligraphy the pages contain. The following names and dates are mentioned: p.1 Shah Mahmud and Mir 'Ali al-Husayni; p.4 Faqir 'Ali; pp.15, 16, 17 Muhammad Salih, dated, on p.15, 1105AH (1693 CE); p.19, Nur al-Din Muhammad al-Isfahani, dated 1087 AH (1676 CE); pp.21, 22, Mir 'Ali, written in Qazwin; p.24 'Abd al-Rashid. Contadini, Anna (ed.), *Objects of Instruction. Treasures of the School of Oriental and African Studies*, London, 2007, p.102 no. 79.

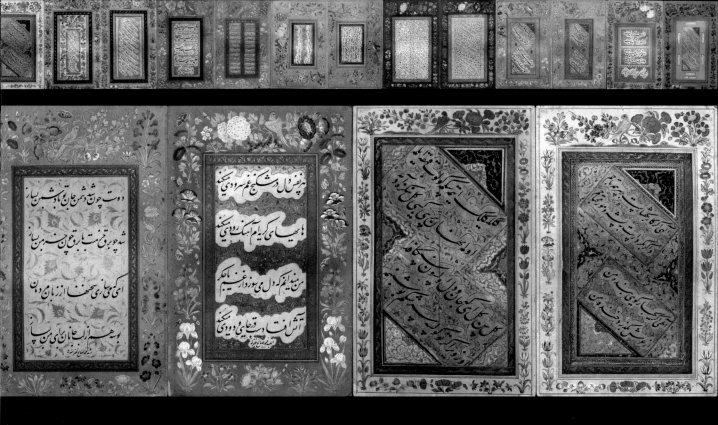

ACKNOWLEDGEMENTS

This exhibition was made possible by the generous curatorial leadership of Rose Issa, a curator, writer and publisher who has championed visual art and film from the Middle East and North Africa in the UK for more than thirty years. It is inspired by her book *Signs of Our Times: From Calligraphy to Calligraffiti*, and her publications and exhibitions of the works of many of the individual artists in the exhibition.

We thank Venetia Porter, British Museum, and SOAS's Anna Contadini (Professor of the History of Islamic Art) and Narguess Farzad (Senior Lecturer in Persian Studies) for their guidance as advisors for the art book section of the exhibition.

Thanks to Francesca Ricci and Petra Kottmair for their editorial and design support in producing the catalogue.

We are indebted to the many artists and private collectors who have lent us works for the exhibition, individually acknowledged in the respective captions.

SOAS's Library Special Collections team have given valuable insights, lent works to the exhibition, provided photographs for this publication and increasingly are making the collection widely available through their ongoing conservation and digitalisation of SOAS's magnificent collection of calligraphy from the Middle East and other regions. Thanks to John Langdon, Mariluz Beltran de Guevara, Erich Kesse and Catherine Buxton.

Dr Claudia Mendias Canale of the SOAS Library provided us with guidance and support throughout, bringing together many colleagues from across SOAS, for which we are grateful. We also thank Angelica Baschiera for her assistance organising the Artists Workshop and events, and Harris Laspas in the SOAS Alumni Engagement office.

Our deep thanks to John Hollingworth, SOAS's Head of Galleries & Exhibitions, a great partner to many curators, who generously shared his expertise and time.

For the sponsorship of the exhibition and this publication, we thank Hani Kalouti of HBK Investments Advisory, Nic and Lindsey Clavel of Scipion Capital SA, Brooke Beardslee and Aziz Takkal of Mid Century Maroc, Dr Edesio Fernandes, and SOAS Library.

BOB ANNIBALE
SENIOR FELLOW
SOAS, UNIVERSITY OF LONDON